Illustrative History in Profanity
First Edition
By Tim Harry, Ian Ford, Ryan Bacchus
Illustrations by LaughterCraft

This book is dedicated to man's ongoing appreciation for history...and humor.

We would like to thank the gracious Kickstarter supporters who made this book possible.

Meet Joe

Our mascot for profanity

This story follows Joe
through the ages.

Right up to present day

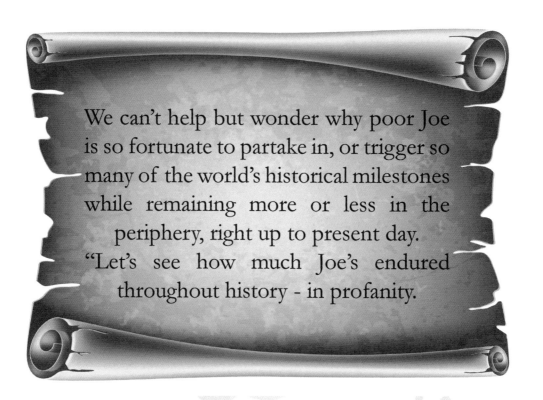

We can't help but wonder why poor Joe is so fortunate to partake in, or trigger so many of the world's historical milestones while remaining more or less in the periphery, right up to present day.

"Let's see how much Joe's endured throughout history - in profanity.

Chapter 1

Before History, Before Man

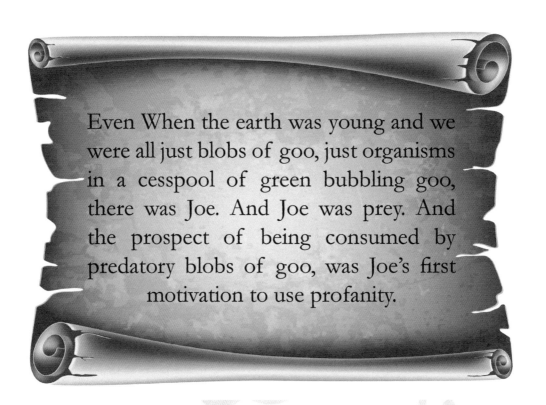

Even When the earth was young and we were all just blobs of goo, just organisms in a cesspool of green bubbling goo, there was Joe. And Joe was prey. And the prospect of being consumed by predatory blobs of goo, was Joe's first motivation to use profanity.

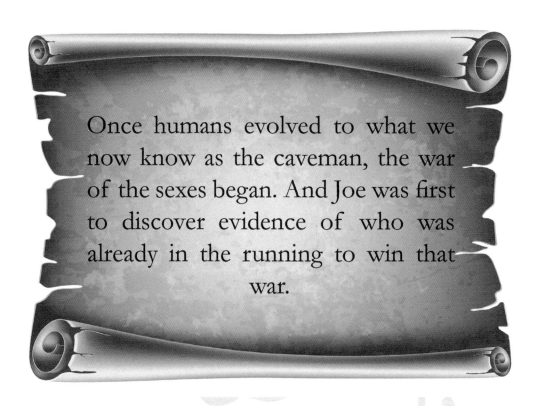

Once humans evolved to what we now know as the caveman, the war of the sexes began. And Joe was first to discover evidence of who was already in the running to win that war.

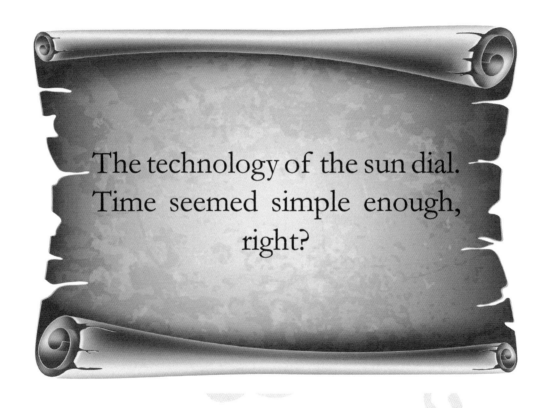

The technology of the sun dial. Time seemed simple enough, right?

Try messing with Stone Henge.

Chapter 2

Classical Antiquity: Ancient Greece and Rome

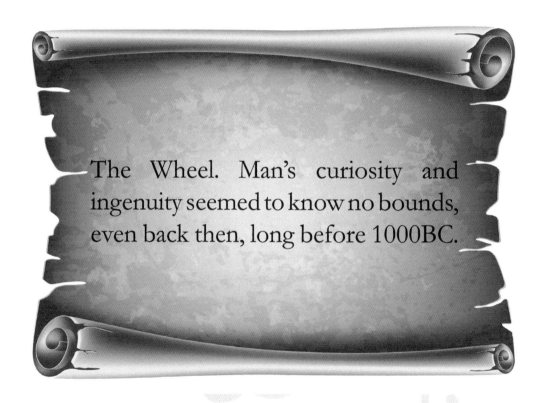

The Wheel. Man's curiosity and ingenuity seemed to know no bounds, even back then, long before 1000BC.

The same can be said for man's competitive nature.

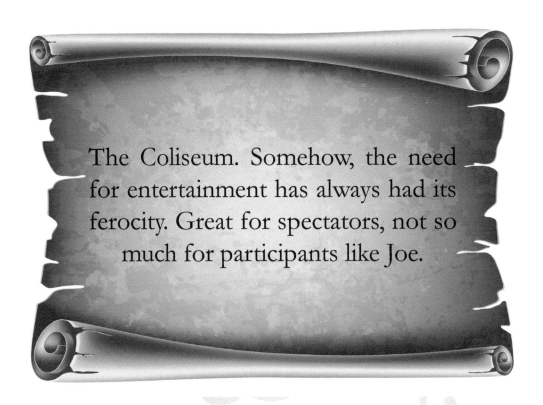

The Coliseum. Somehow, the need for entertainment has always had its ferocity. Great for spectators, not so much for participants like Joe.

Julius Caesar. A man of great vision and wisdom, on a quest for knowledge, progress and power. As he crosses the Rubicon in an attempt to conquor Rome, he pronounces they would take an 'all hands on deck' approach to their impending battle. Inspiring for his courageous army. Not so much for Joe.

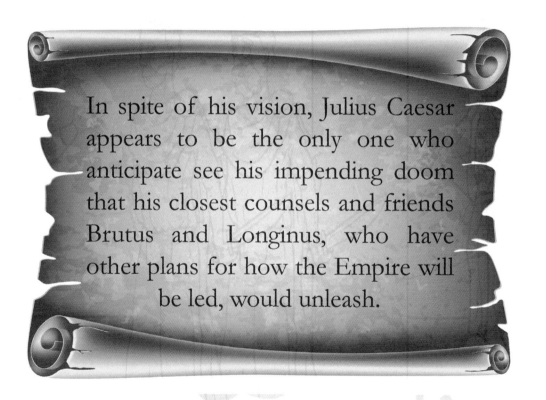

In spite of his vision, Julius Caesar appears to be the only one who anticipate see his impending doom that his closest counsels and friends Brutus and Longinus, who have other plans for how the Empire will be led, would unleash.

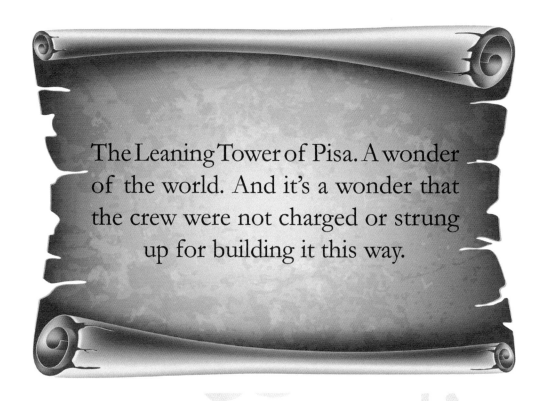

The Leaning Tower of Pisa. A wonder of the world. And it's a wonder that the crew were not charged or strung up for building it this way.

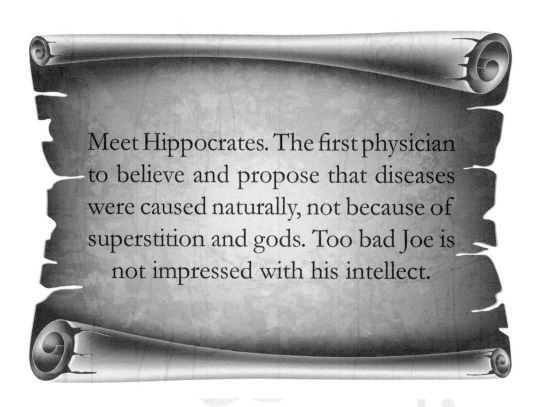

Meet Hippocrates. The first physician to believe and propose that diseases were caused naturally, not because of superstition and gods. Too bad Joe is not impressed with his intellect.

Chapter 3

China and The East: So Many Dynasties

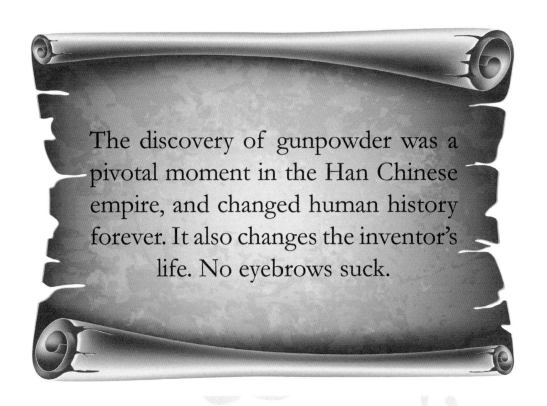

The discovery of gunpowder was a pivotal moment in the Han Chinese empire, and changed human history forever. It also changes the inventor's life. No eyebrows suck.

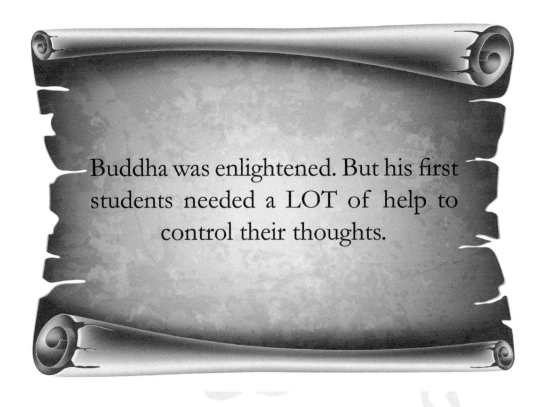

Buddha was enlightened. But his first students needed a LOT of help to control their thoughts.

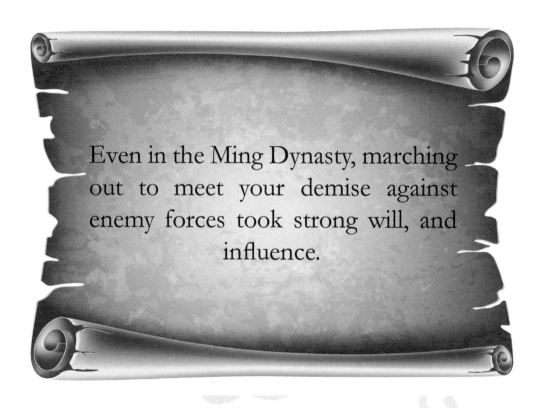

Even in the Ming Dynasty, marching out to meet your demise against enemy forces took strong will, and influence.

Chapter 4

Egypt and the Persian Empire

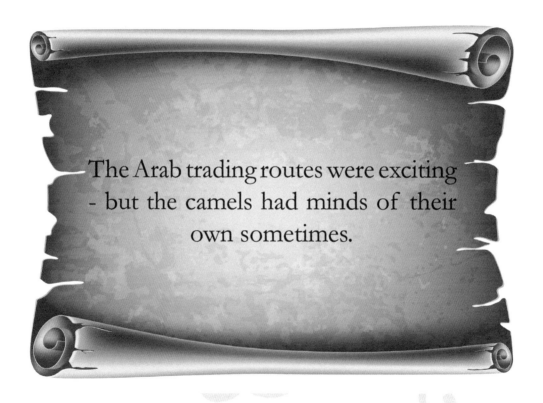

The Arab trading routes were exciting - but the camels had minds of their own sometimes.

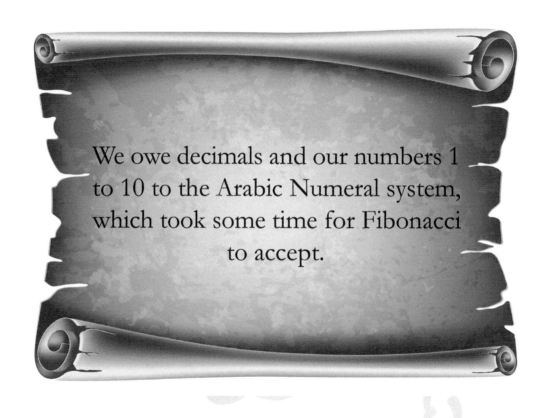

We owe decimals and our numbers 1 to 10 to the Arabic Numeral system, which took some time for Fibonacci to accept.

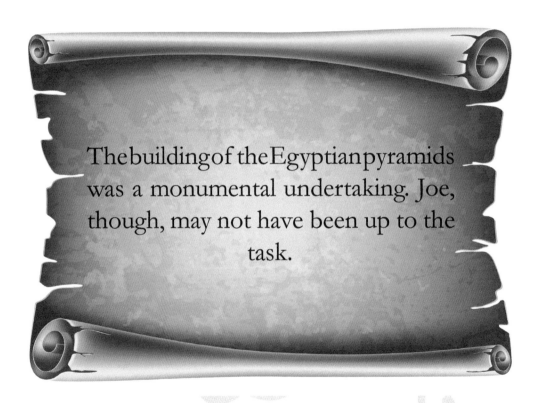

The building of the Egyptian pyramids was a monumental undertaking. Joe, though, may not have been up to the task.

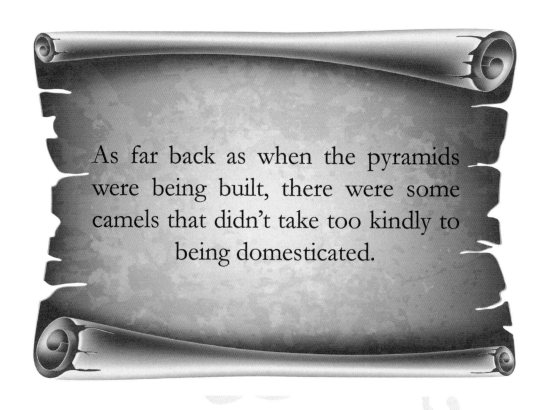

As far back as when the pyramids were being built, there were some camels that didn't take too kindly to being domesticated.

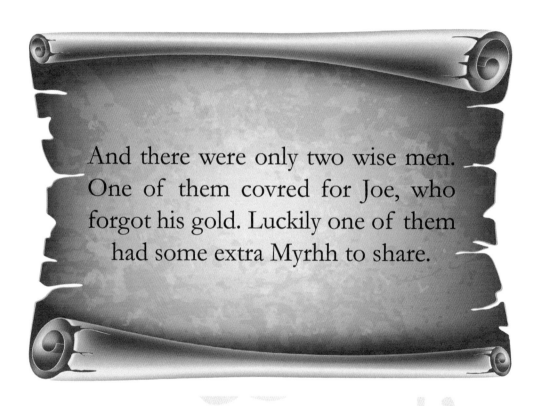

And there were only two wise men. One of them covred for Joe, who forgot his gold. Luckily one of them had some extra Myrhh to share.

Chapter 5

Our Esteemed Guest Illustrators

Illustrator Joel Ferris

In 1953, construction began on a chapel to commemorate The Battle of Little Bighorn and Custer's Last Stand. Salvador Dalí was commissioned to paint a mural within the sanctuary. Dalí locked himself away in the unfinished church for several weeks to work in secret. Dalí sent word to the clergy that he was prepared to reveal his mural. When Dalí pulled the curtain, all they saw was a monumental pile of feces, topped with a halo and surrounded by a mob of native Americans squirming in a surreal orientation. The priest screamed, "What is this?" Dalí answered, "Custer's last words: 'Holy $#!p! Look at all those ‡µ©=!v% Indians! Construction on the chapel was never completed.

Merde sainte! Regarde tous ces fichus Indiens!

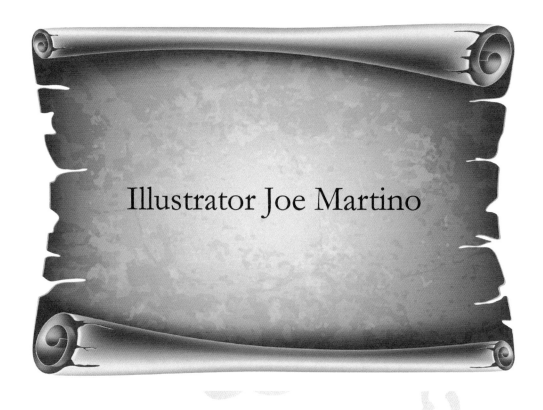

Illustrator Joe Martino

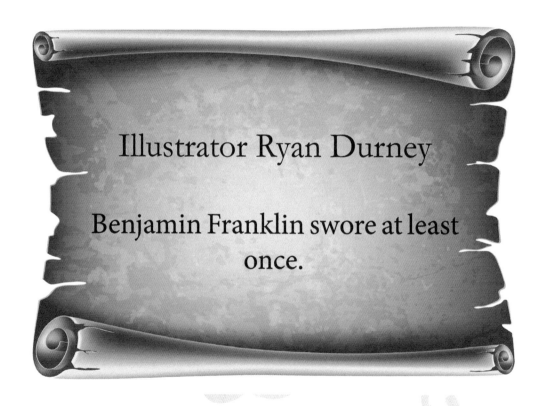

Illustrator Ryan Durney

Benjamin Franklin swore at least once.

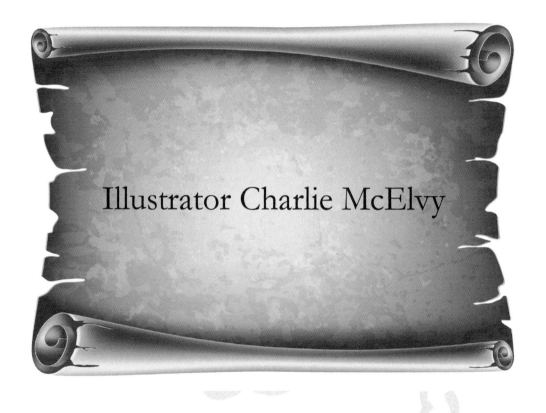

Illustrator Charlie McElvy

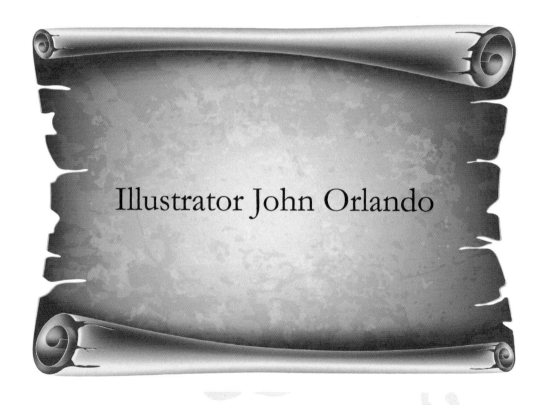

Illustrator John Orlando

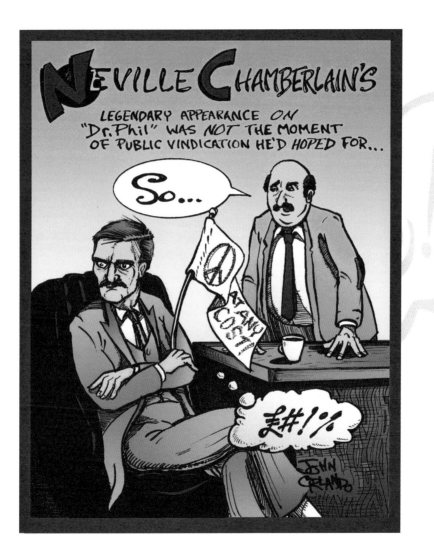

72

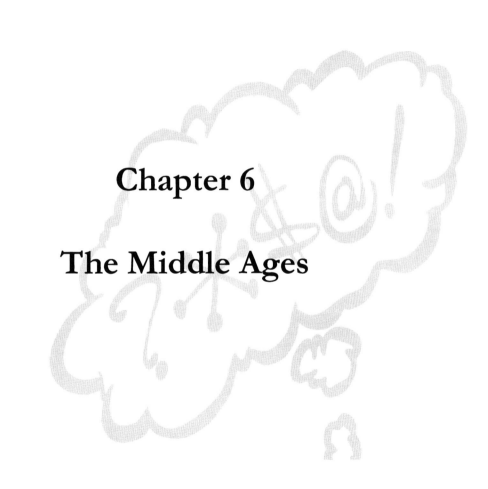

Chapter 6

The Middle Ages

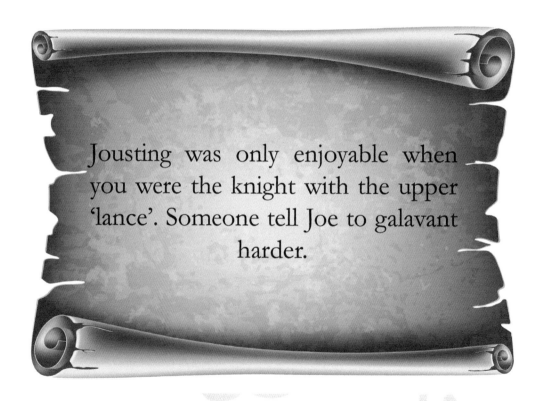

Jousting was only enjoyable when you were the knight with the upper 'lance'. Someone tell Joe to galavant harder.

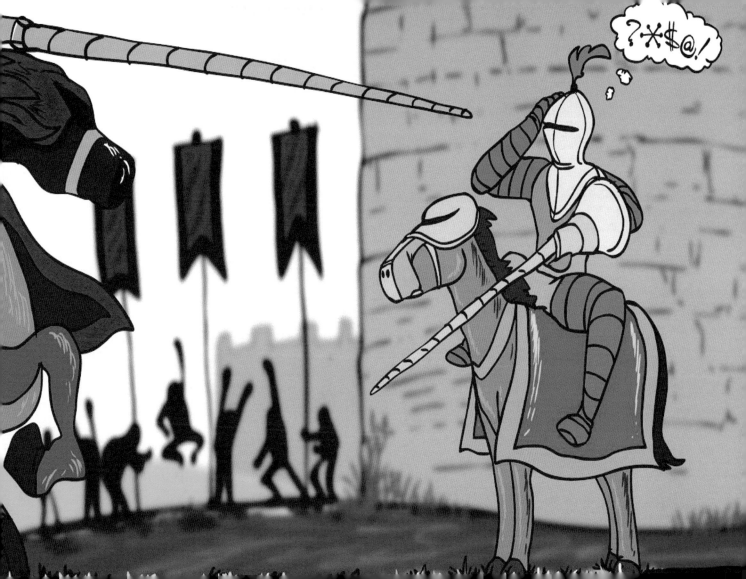

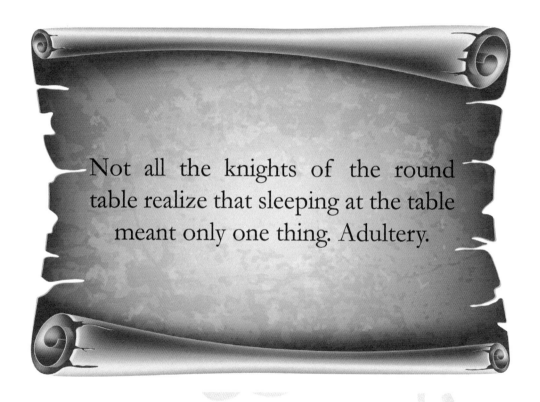

Not all the knights of the round table realize that sleeping at the table meant only one thing. Adultery.

Yes. The fashion police was ready to give its first set of advice. Rule #1: When being knighted, do wear the right attire.

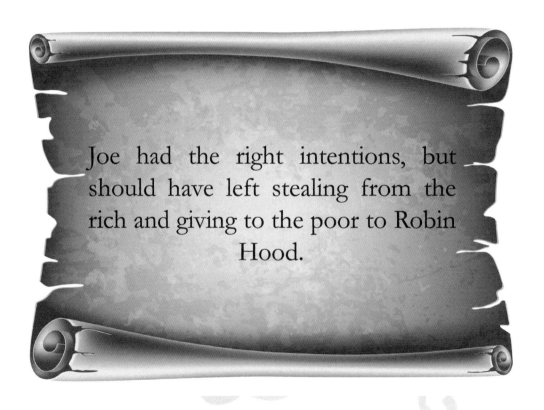

Joe had the right intentions, but should have left stealing from the rich and giving to the poor to Robin Hood.

Chapter 7

The Age of Exploration and the Renaissance

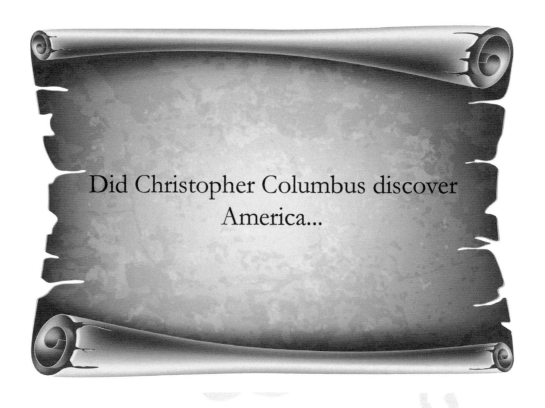

Did Christopher Columbus discover America...

...or did the first Americans discover him?

Romeo needs GPS. Romeo must die.

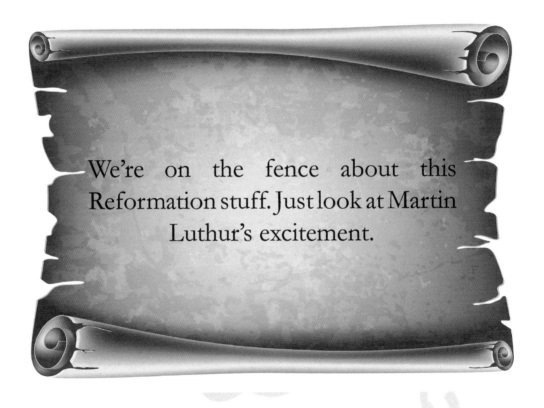

We're on the fence about this Reformation stuff. Just look at Martin Luthur's excitement.

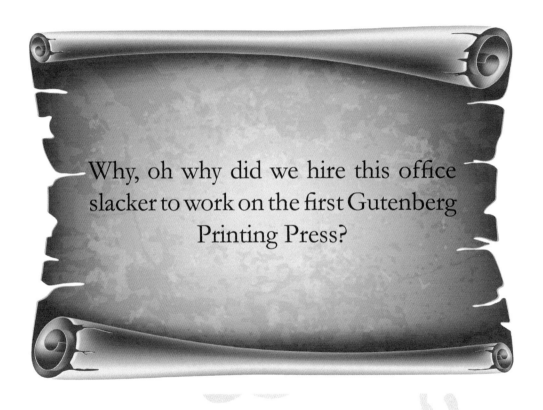

Why, oh why did we hire this office slacker to work on the first Gutenberg Printing Press?

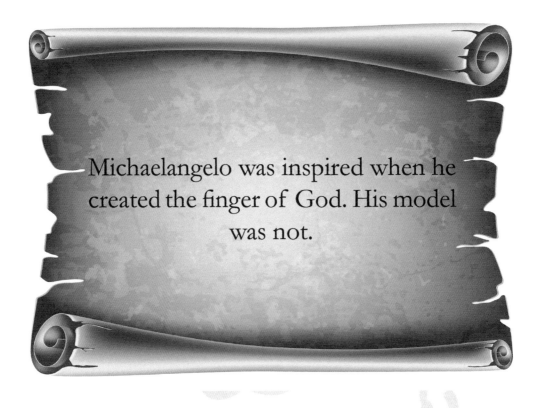

Michaelangelo was inspired when he created the finger of God. His model was not.

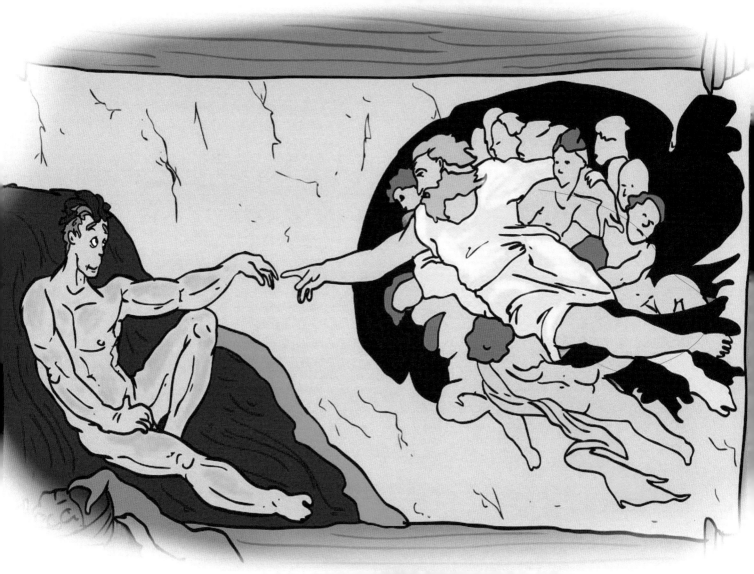

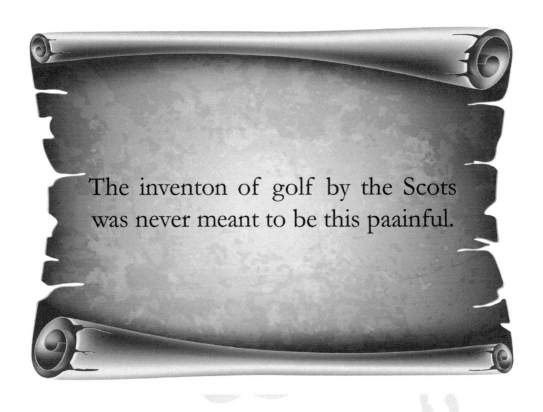

The inventon of golf by the Scots was never meant to be this paainful.

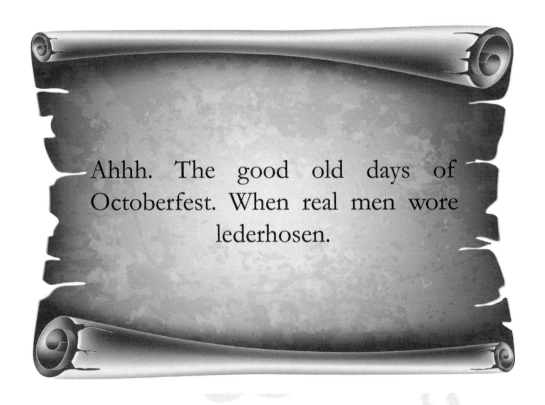

Ahhh. The good old days of Octoberfest. When real men wore lederhosen.

Chapter 8

Age of Revolution

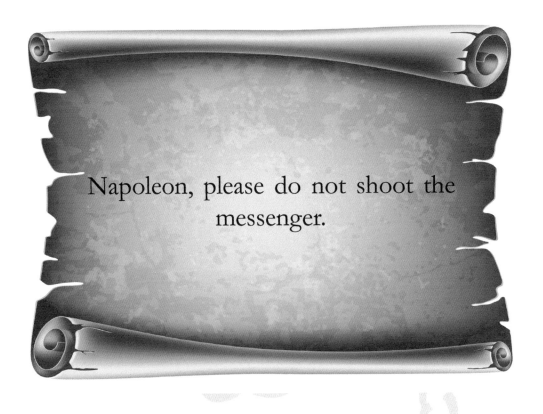

Napoleon, please do not shoot the messenger.

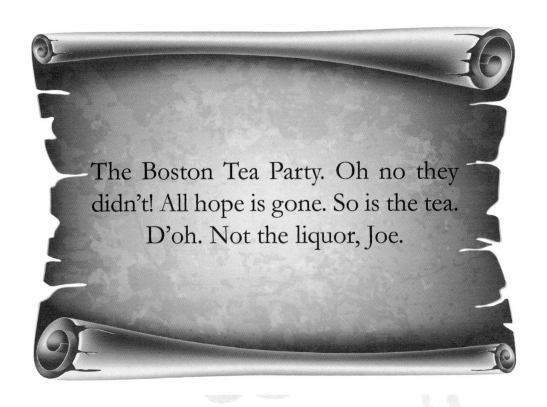

The Boston Tea Party. Oh no they didn't! All hope is gone. So is the tea. D'oh. Not the liquor, Joe.

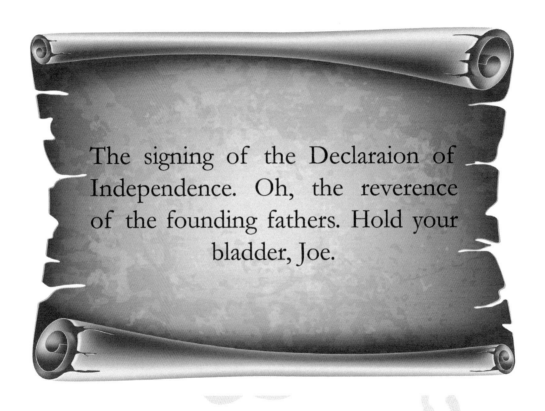

The signing of the Declaraion of Independence. Oh, the reverence of the founding fathers. Hold your bladder, Joe.

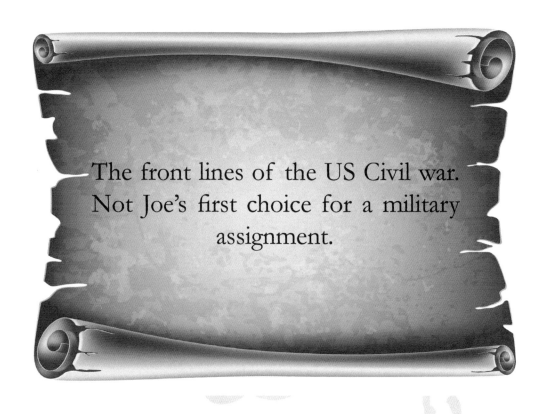

The front lines of the US Civil war. Not Joe's first choice for a military assignment.

Chapter 9

The Industrial Age and Other Firsts

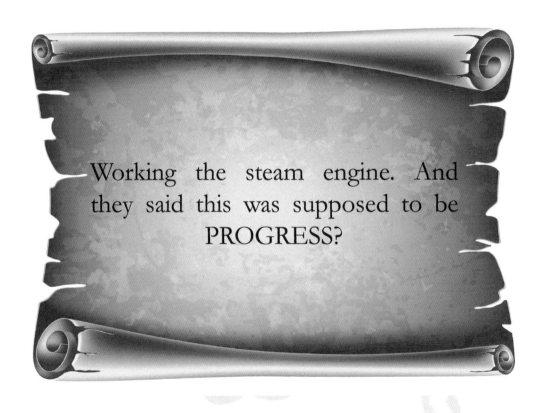

Working the steam engine. And they said this was supposed to be PROGRESS?

Well, at least Joe gets to fashion cool tools.

Steampunk never looks this exciting.

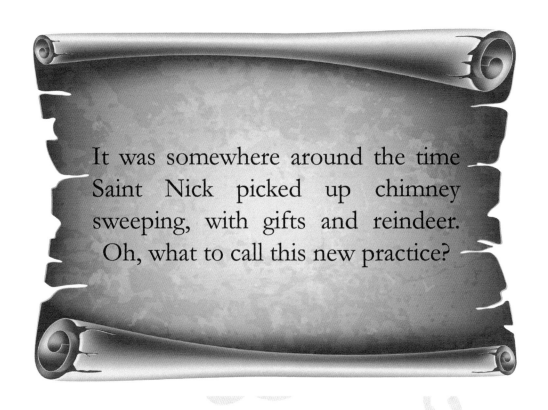

It was somewhere around the time Saint Nick picked up chimney sweeping, with gifts and reindeer. Oh, what to call this new practice?

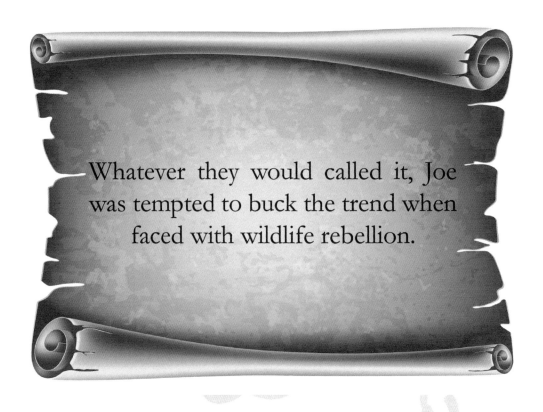

Whatever they would called it, Joe was tempted to buck the trend when faced with wildlife rebellion.

Chapter 10

Contemporary History
An Oxymoron? You tell me...

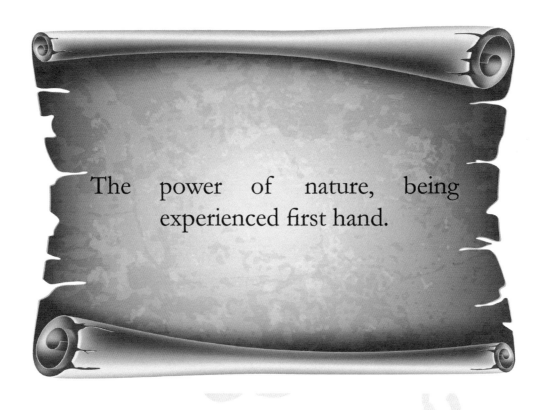

The power of nature, being experienced first hand.

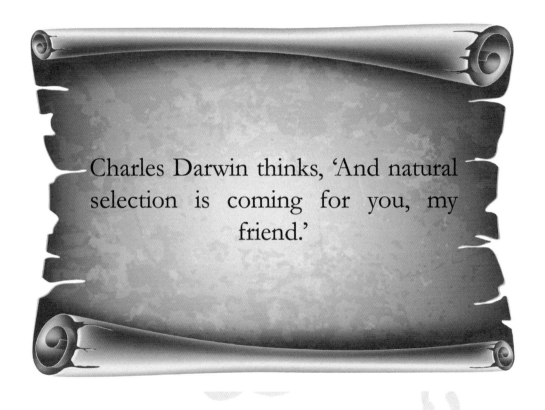

Charles Darwin thinks, 'And natural selection is coming for you, my friend.'

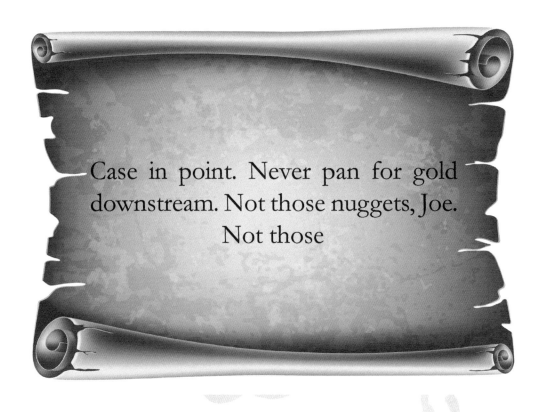

Case in point. Never pan for gold downstream. Not those nuggets, Joe. Not those

Balloon rides. Oh, for the love of height.

The Wright Brothers. For the love of flight.

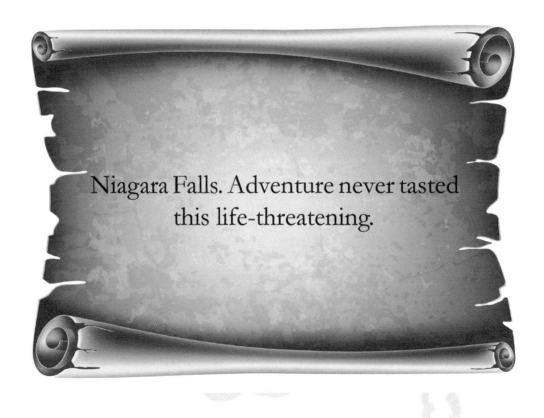

Niagara Falls. Adventure never tasted this life-threatening.

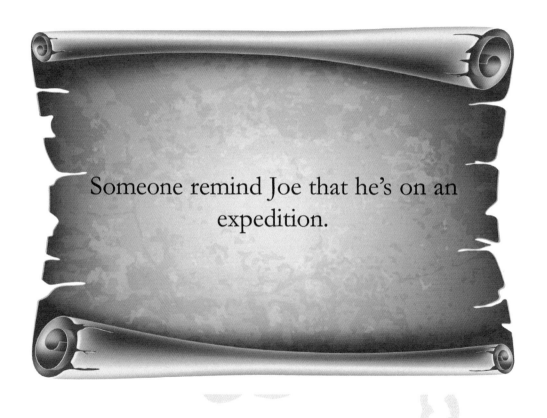

Someone remind Joe that he's on an expedition.

Good going, Sherlock.

Chapter 11

The Rise of Modern War

From the air...

To the trenches...

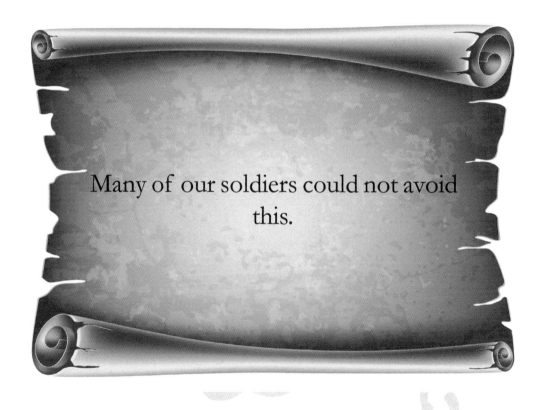

Many of our soldiers could not avoid this.

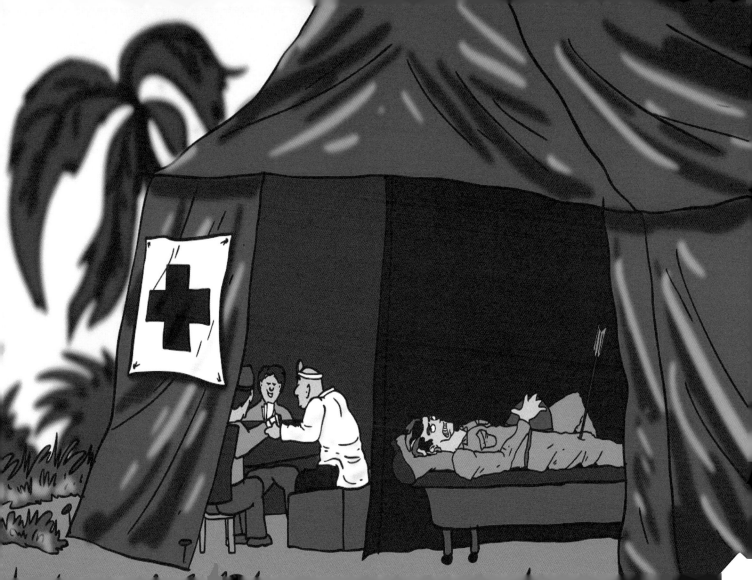

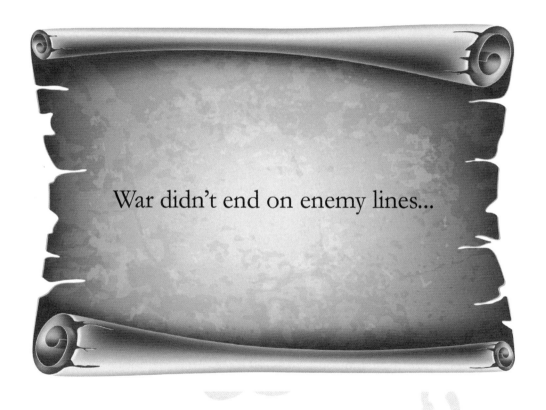

War didn't end on enemy lines...

Chapter 12

The Sixties. Oh My.

Free love...

Still had consequences.

Venice vacations were all the rage.

Man made it to the moon.

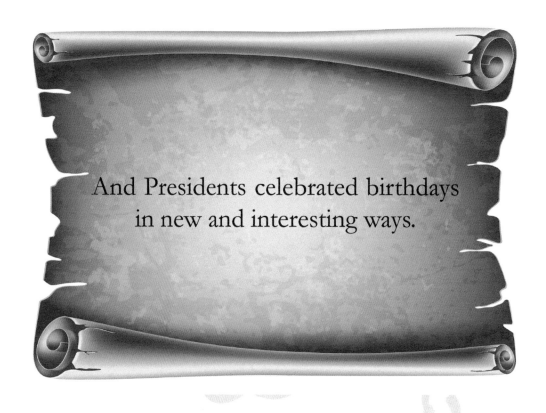

And Presidents celebrated birthdays
in new and interesting ways.

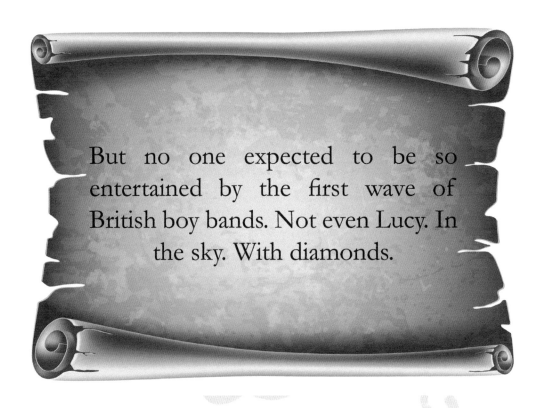

But no one expected to be so entertained by the first wave of British boy bands. Not even Lucy. In the sky. With diamonds.

164

Chapter 13

The Eighties to Present Day Breakthroughs.

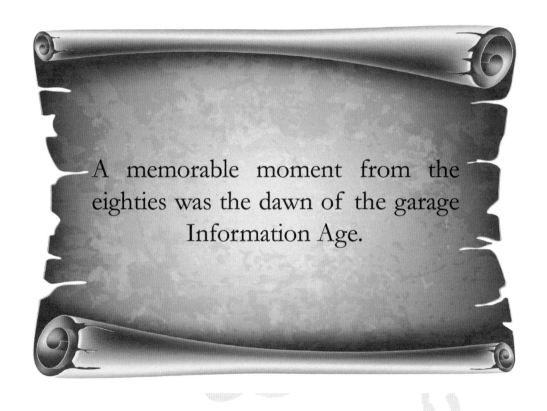

A memorable moment from the eighties was the dawn of the garage Information Age.

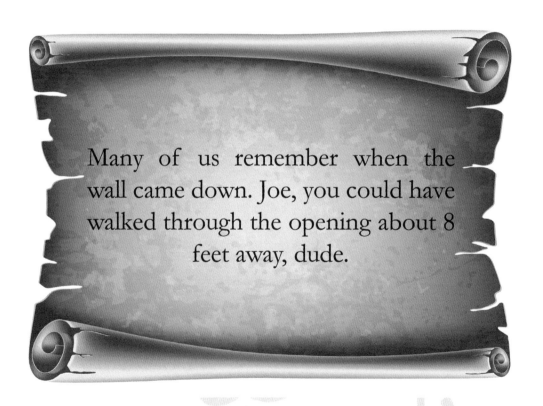

Many of us remember when the wall came down. Joe, you could have walked through the opening about 8 feet away, dude.

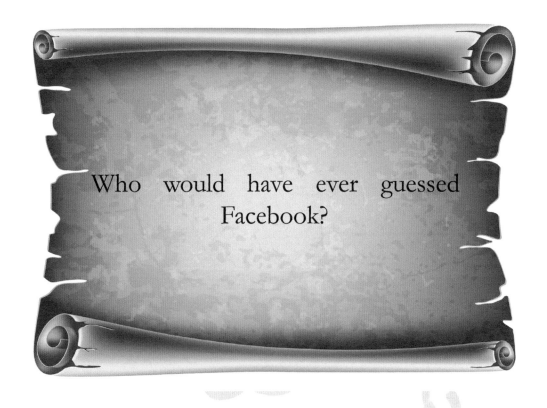

Who would have ever guessed Facebook?

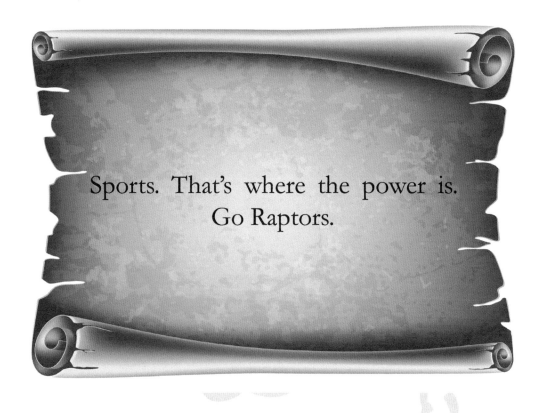

Sports. That's where the power is. Go Raptors.

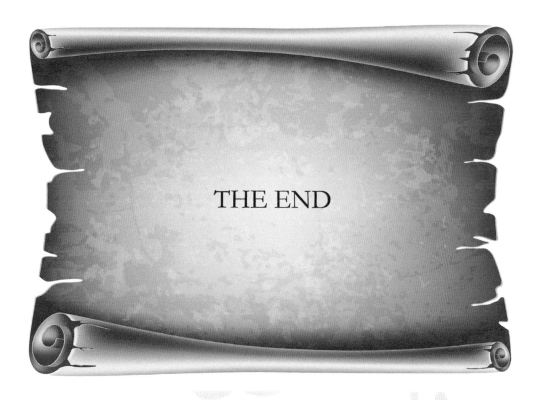

THE END

Made in the USA
Charleston, SC
21 November 2015